Best Inventions

Toilet

by Julie Murray

Dash!
LEVELED READERS

An Imprint of Abdo Zoom • abdobooks.com

3 Dash! LEVELED READERS

Level 1 – Beginning
Short and simple sentences with familiar words or patterns for children who are beginning to understand how letters and sounds go together.

Level 2 – Emerging
Longer words and sentences with more complex language patterns for readers who are practicing common words and letter sounds.

Level 3 – Transitional
More developed language and vocabulary for readers who are becoming more independent.

THIS BOOK CONTAINS RECYCLED MATERIALS

abdobooks.com

Published by Abdo Zoom, a division of ABDO, PO Box 398166, Minneapolis, Minnesota 55439.

Printed in the United States of America, North Mankato, Minnesota.
102022
012023

Photo Credits: Alamy, Getty Images, Shutterstock
Production Contributors: Kenny Abdo, Jennie Forsberg, Grace Hansen, John Hansen
Design Contributors: Candice Keimig, Neil Klinepier, Colleen McLaren

Library of Congress Control Number: 2022937310

Publisher's Cataloging in Publication Data

Names: Murray, Julie, author.
Title: Toilet / by Julie Murray
Description: Minneapolis, Minnesota : Abdo Zoom, 2023 | Series: Best inventions | Includes online resources and index.
Identifiers: ISBN 9781098280208 (lib. bdg.) | ISBN 9781098280734 (ebook) | ISBN 9781098281038 (Read-to-Me ebook)
Subjects: LCSH: Toilets--History--Juvenile literature. | Inventions--Juvenile literature. | Sanitation--Juvenile literature. | Inventions--History--Juvenile literature.
Classification: DDC 696.182--dc23

Table of Contents

Toilet

Toilets date back as early as 3100 BCE. The earliest known toilet was found at Skara Brae, a **Neolithic** settlement. It is located on the Orkney Islands of Scotland.

The **Mesopotamians** further developed the toilet. They had sitting toilets.

They also created a sewer system using water to drain waste into clay pipes.

8

By 300 CE the Romans had created communal toilets. Holes were carved every few feet into long stone benches. Waste flowed into a channel. This connected to a sewer system.

For hundreds of years, Europeans disposed of their waste in **chutes** that led to the street.

Chamber pots were also dumped out of windows. This created a stinky mess and **unsanitary** conditions!

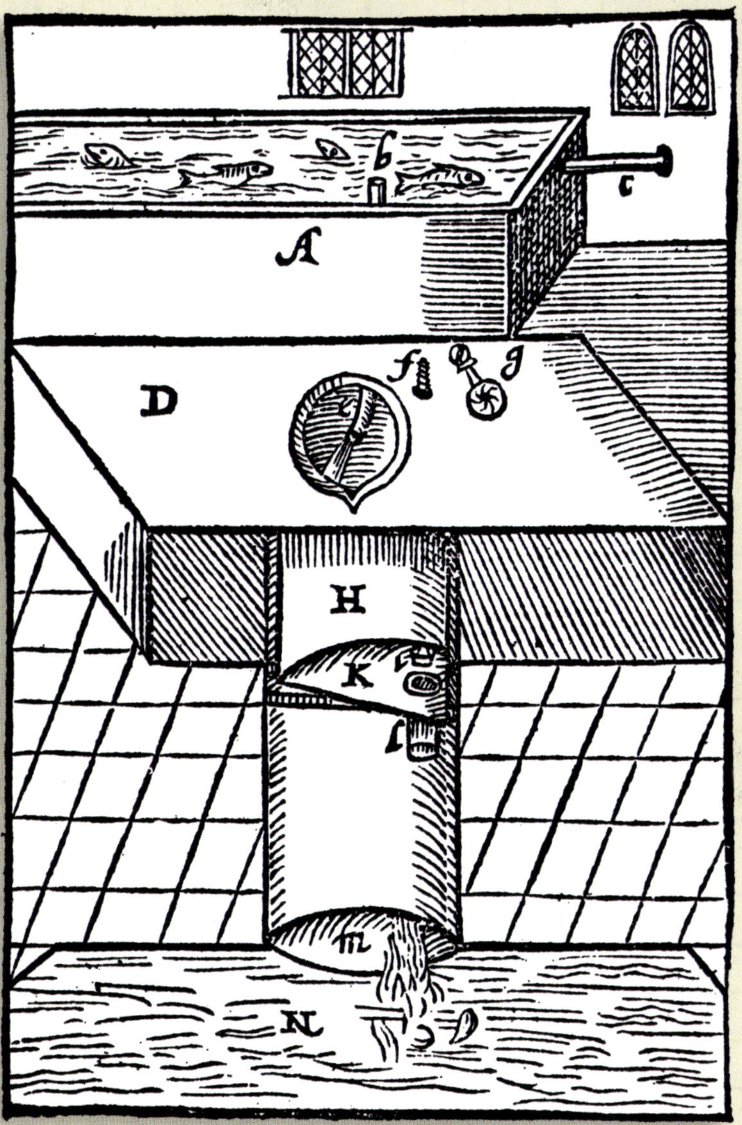

In 1596, Sir John Harington invented the flush toilet. He named it Ajax. He made one for Queen Elizabeth I. It did not become common until 1851.

Toilets Today

Today, toilets are quite comfortable and easy to use. Some toilets are high-tech. They can self-flush, light up, and even play music!

How A Flush Toilet Works

Using the handle to flush the toilet lifts a flapper in the tank. This releases tank water into the bowl. As the tank empties, a float lowers.

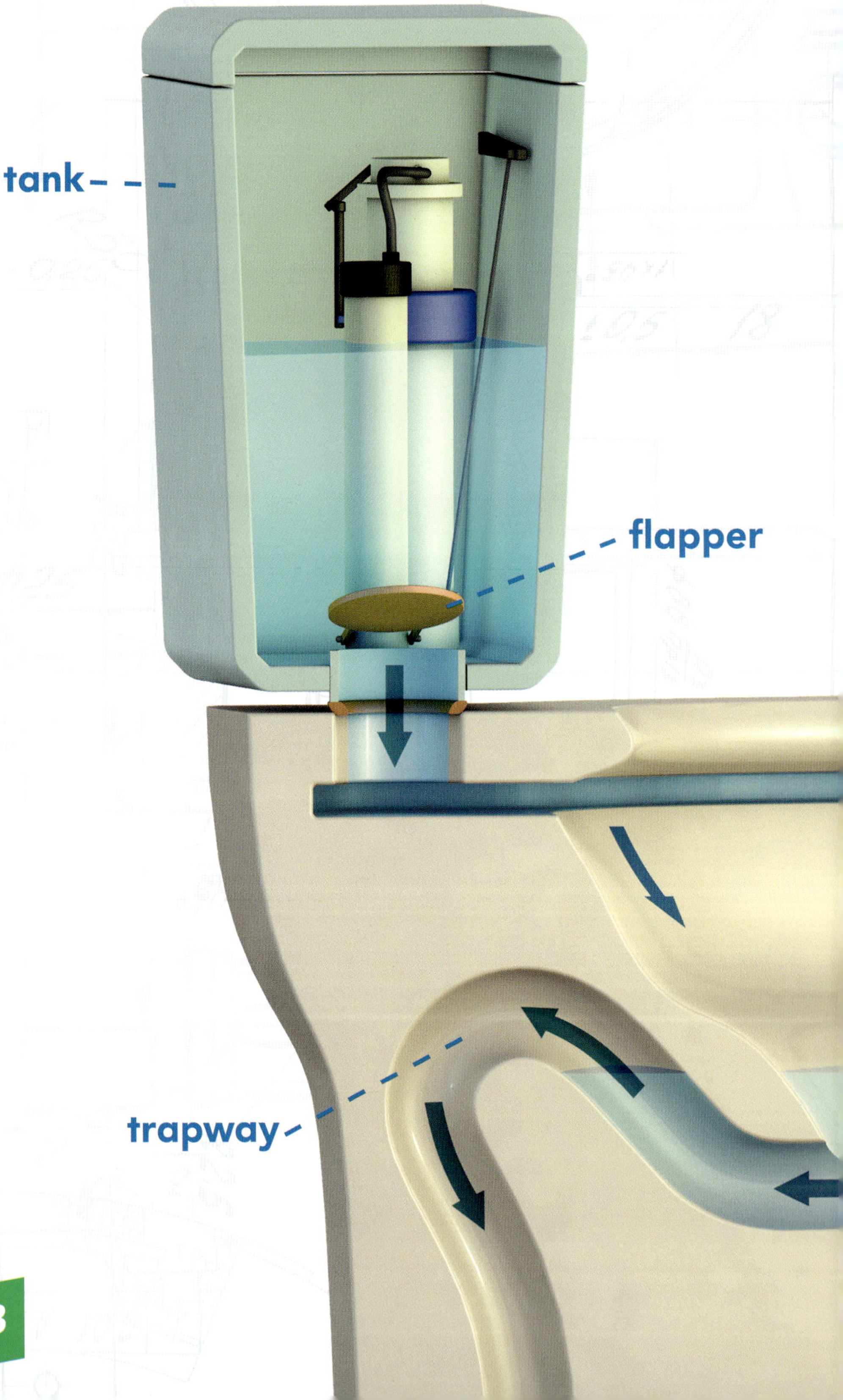
tank
flapper
trapway

Gravity forces water into the trapway, which creates suction. The water and waste are sucked out of the bowl and into drainage pipes. These pipes lead to a sewer system.

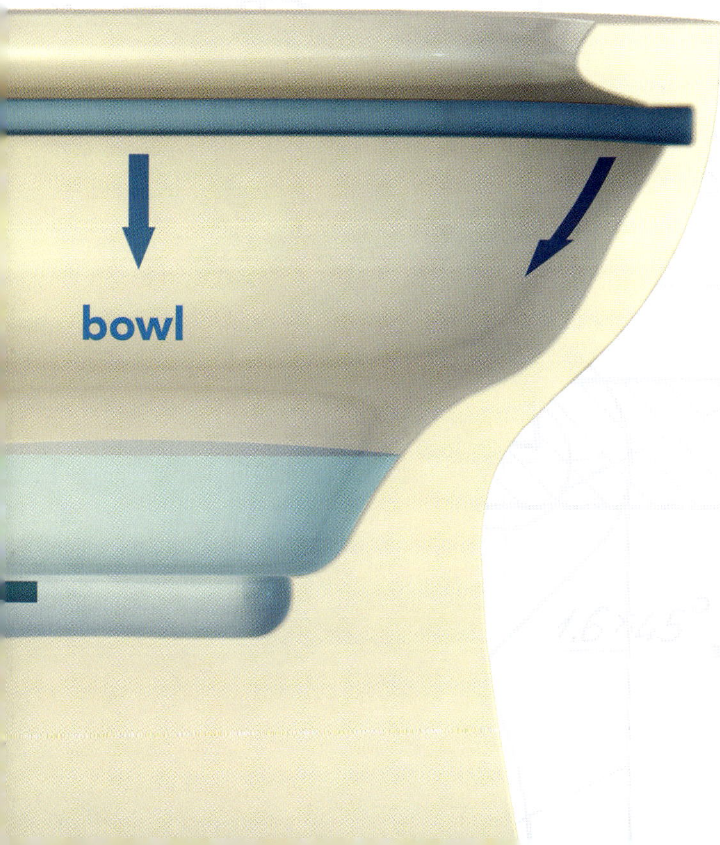

Lastly, air enters the trapway and the suction stops. Water drains back into the tank from the fill valve.

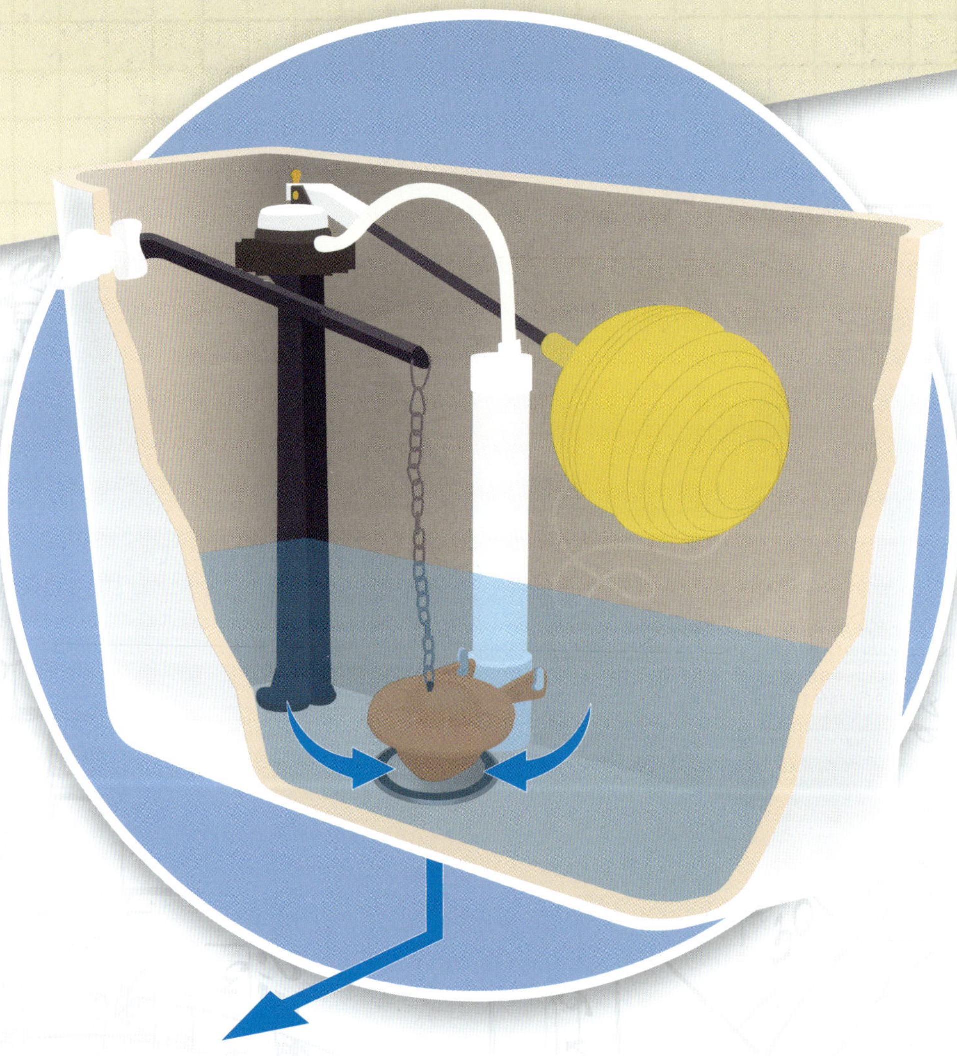

flapper valve open

It lifts the float until it shuts off the fill valve. This keeps the water from running.

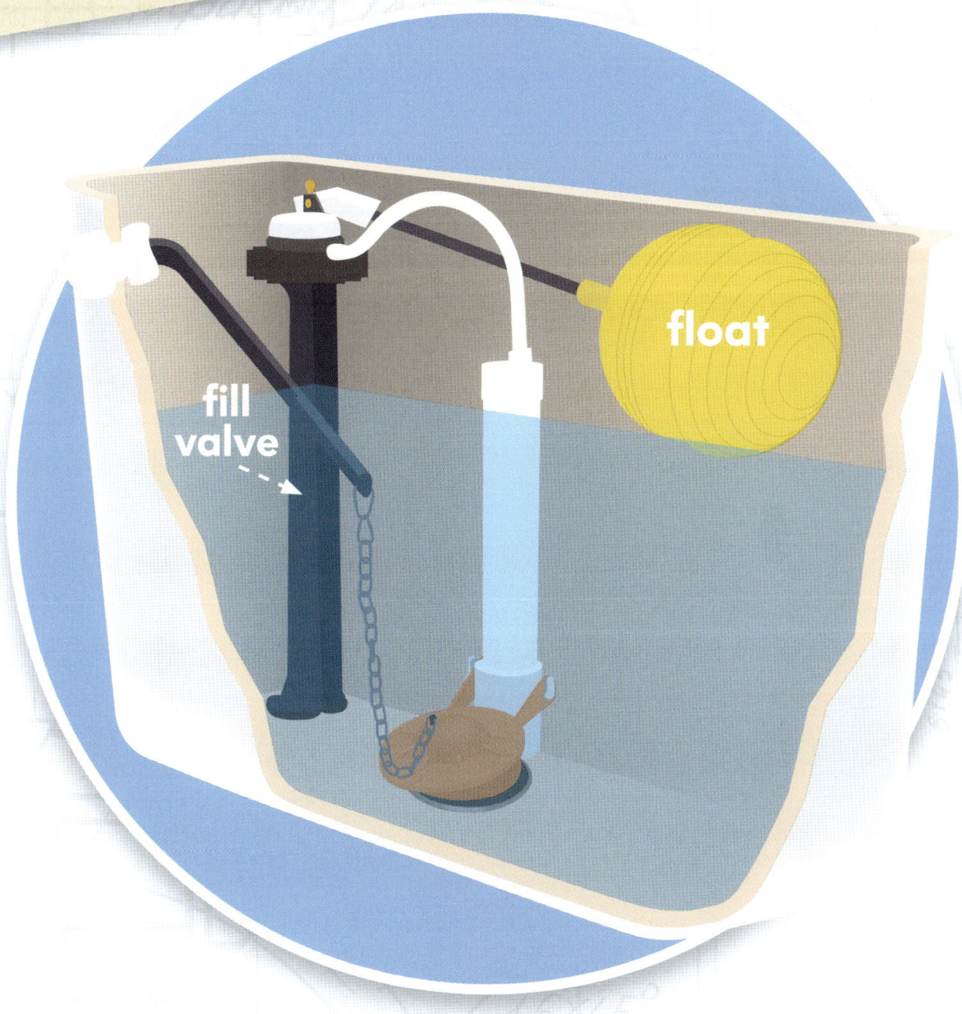

full water tank

More Facts

- The first toilet to appear on television was in *Leave It to Beaver* in 1957.
- About 4.5 billion people around the world do not have access to a toilet that safely disposes of waste.
- The most expensive toilet system is in space. The bathroom on the **International Space Station** cost $23 million!

Glossary

chamber pot – a bowl kept in a bedroom and used as a toilet at night.

chute – a passage down which things may slide to be moved from one area to another.

International Space Station – a laboratory in space that orbits Earth. Astronauts from around the world live and work there.

Mesopotamian – a person who lived in Mesopotamia, a region in southwestern Asia that is thought to be one of the places where early civilization developed.

Neolithic – relating to the time period near the end of the Stone Age when a wide-ranging set of developments appeared, such as tools and polished stone weapons.

unsanitary – unclean.

Index

Online Resources

Booklinks
NONFICTION NETWORK
FREE! ONLINE NONFICTION RESOURCES

To learn more about toilets, please visit **abdobooklinks.com** or scan this QR code. These links are routinely monitored and updated to provide the most current information available.